THE OAKLAND PARAMOUNT

THE OAKLAND
PARAMOUNT

Text by Susannah Harris Stone
Photographs by Roger Minick
Preface by Peter Botto

For Jim Roseveare,
the Paramount's first staff organist,
without whom the Paramount seems
a good deal emptier.

Preface

When Jack Bethards, Executive Director of the Oakland Symphony, asked me to manage the Paramount and its restoration project, I said I didn't think I was interested. My career was heading in other directions. But I hadn't seen the Paramount yet. I finally had to agree to look at the place before he would take my "no" for an answer. That was in October 1972, and so much for my other career. Almost 10 years later, I still haven't found another project challenging enough to lure me away from the Paramount.

Recalling my part of the restoration project for this book has been fun and it has reminded me how exciting that job was. Architecturally, the Paramount was a huge success when it first opened in 1931, and we were determined to adhere faithfully to the building's original design. Who would even dream of changing any aspect of Pflueger's perfect Art Deco fantasy? Well, during the restoration some people thought their decorating skills exceeded those of the architect's. But with Jack handling the political front, and Steve Levin, President of the Theatre Historical Society, authenticating details, we fought off proposals for modern, red auditorium chairs, blue carpet, white walls with gold trim, a gold grand drape, new furniture and wall paintings selected by committee. A glance through the photographs in this book illustrates how contrary those ideas would have been to the Paramount!

The effect we wanted was to return the building exactly to the way it looked at its grand opening, duplicating every detail from overall color schemes of walls, carpets and furniture down to the colors of the mechanical equipment locked away in the basement. And we did.

In 1931, the Paramount Publix director for the Paramount project was Nathan Light, who, a few years after the restoration, returned to tour the theater. As the old gentleman's eyes lovingly passed over the building that surely represented one of the most important achievements of his lifetime, he remarked, "It's amazing how well the building's been maintained!" No other comment could have been more satisfying to verify the authenticity of the million-dollar project. In recognition of the building's status as a rare survivor from the era of the movie palace, and for its outstanding Art Deco architecture and decor, the Paramount was designated a National Historic Landmark in 1977, and was one of the youngest buildings ever to attain that status.

But the project goes on. Since reopening in September 1973, we've installed the mighty Wurlitzer, thus *really* completing the restoration; we've taken care to protect the irreplaceable interior by waterproofing most of the building's exterior; and we've modernized the stage and auditorium lighting controls, as well as the air conditioning system, to fill the needs of modern events and audiences—all without making any changes in the theater's appearance. In fact, the Paramount is impeccably (some say fanatically) maintained so that newcomers, unexpectedly transported by the Paramount's Art Deco paradise, gaze with open mouths and wondering eyes just as those did opening night in 1931. Much of the pleasure of being associated with the Paramount is derived from the appreciation of others.

Of course, the doors would not have opened at all without those who made the Paramount project possible: Jack Bethards and Steve Levin; Harry Lange—who, as President of the Oakland Symphony, initiated the Paramount's restoration; Joe and Dee Knowland—project fund raisers; John Reading and Wally Carroll—Oakland city officials; the late Anthony Heinsbergen—decorator; and Milton Pflueger, who has given invaluable research assistance, both during the restoration and in the writing of this book.

I'm so delighted with the way Susannah Stone has told the Paramount story—and Roger Minick's

photographs are fabulous. There've been a number of picture books published in the last several years on old movie palaces—some very nice. But one problem they all possess is their inaccuracy: a wrong credit here, a mis-identified photograph there. That is not the case with this book. First-hand information was obtained from the original architect's firm and from those involved with the restoration, and then the work was reviewed for accuracy before going to press. We are much in debt to publisher Dick Schuettge, and to Susannah and Roger, for telling the Paramount story so accurately and beautifully.

I have to say, though, that this book does not tell the whole story. No book could. You have to see the Paramount in person to fully appreciate it. But if a visit is out of the question, we hope this book will convey the Paramount's magic to you.

– Peter Botto
Oakland, California
1981

BRIGHT LIGHTS
AND DARK YEARS:

The History of the Paramount

Were the Paramount to require a new name, it might well be called the Paradox, for its history is studded with contradictions. It is a motion-picture palace where motion pictures are now seldom shown; and it is a gilded fantasy that was brought to life in the midst of Depression-era poverty. Apparently doomed, shortly after its completion, to a long slow downhill slide toward ultimate destruc-tion, it has instead been restored to its original splendor, christened a national landmark, and turned into a vital, brilliant theater for the performing arts.

At the time of its construction, the Paramount's destiny seemed clear. It was to be one of the world's most modern and magnificent combination (movie-vaudeville) houses; and, in a time of economic

woe, it was to be a great boon to the city of Oakland in a number of ways. It would boost the local building-supply industry and add to the city's prestige. It would draw theatergoers from the entire surrounding area. More important, it would provide jobs.

"Work Here For Idle Men," said the headlines that described the groundbreaking, which took place on December 11, 1930. "Steam Shovel Sounds Knell of Bad Times." The steam shovel's knell had in fact sounded ten days earlier, on December 1, when actual construction began. The groundbreaking was a civic ceremony staged by the chamber of commerce as a statement to the builders that Oakland appreciated their business, and as an assurance to worried citizens that there was hope for the future and even for the present. A gold-plated shovel was used to lift the symbolic first spadeful of earth, and there were speeches, bands, a parade. The news stories described a festive event, but the pictures were more sober: photographs of a sea of solemn, hatted men thronged around a speakers' platform that was rough-looking but draped with hopeful bunting. "Local Labor Employed In The Building Of Great Moving Picture Palace," the next day's headlines asserted.

Palace was both a common and an accurate term for the movie theaters of the 1920s and early '30s. They were also called *castles, temples,* and *shrines.* The Roxy, in New York, was advertised as "The Cathedral of the Motion Picture" when it opened in 1927. And across the bay from Oakland, the lavish San Francisco Fox, built in 1929, was being billed as an *art institute of amusements.* "You enter the wide swinging doors of this great Castle of Splendor," its brochure said,

> and behold: The silent magic of life's mirror, the Screen, in creations of its finest magicians; . . .the thousand throated organ, now whispering in gentle melody, now reverberating in mighty thunder; . . .the Orchestra, trained musicians, fingers of the soul of genius, in caprice of syncopation, in mysteries and moods of exquisite harmony; . . .a myriad of multi-colored lights, . . .architectural beauties; . . .soft miles of carpeted wonder in lounge and foyer, in lobby and orchestra, in loge and balcony; . . .Aladdin-like elevators that gently whisk you to balcony, and back again; . . .the vast magnificence of the palace of a King; . . .the swift and silent service of courteous minute-men, couriers of ushering attention. Not King, nor Emperor, nor Croesus could command more!

It was the inflated language of the Roaring Twenties, so soon to roar into a Depression for which no one was prepared. But it tells us now of a brief period when movies enjoyed both the status of the opera and the audiences of the circus—when a cultural and artistic medium had been discovered that could fascinate anyone, and when the houses of royalty were copied and even outdone for the satisfaction of the common man and woman.

The Paramount was among the last of these cinema-castle extravaganzas to be built (Radio City Music Hall, which opened a year later, was the last), and it was erected as part of a theater-chain construction program that had begun in 1925 with the building of the New York Paramount by Paramount Publix Corporation, the theater division of Paramount Pictures. It is often said that the Paramount's opulence was intended to distract poverty- and trouble-ridden patrons from their fears, and certainly this is true; even before the stock market crash of 1929, film studios were prescribing their products as an antidote to "cares and worries." But it was also hoped that continued industry and

optimism would buoy the economy from what was thought to be a temporary slump, and the Paramount's groundbreaking was greeted by the *Oakland Post Enquirer* as "a knockout for pessimism, for gloomy doubt."

For the design of the nationwide chain of Paramount theaters, the Chicago partnership of Rapp & Rapp was the architectural firm most often chosen. But local architects too were considered and sometimes selected, and for the Oakland Paramount, Publix Corporation turned to the San Francisco company of Miller & Pflueger.

It was a serendipitous choice. Pflueger was one of San Francisco's most colorful artistic figures, and monuments to his extraordinary style and unusual eclecticism are scattered throughout the Bay Area. Fans of old movie theaters may recognize him as the architect of the Castro, Alhambra, and El Rey theaters in San Francisco, but he is better known as the designer of the Pacific Coast Stock Exchange, I. Magnin's on Union Square and the Union Square Garage (the world's first underground parking garage), S.F. City College, Washington High School, and Roosevelt Junior High. With the end of Prohibition, he became the creator of a new kind of entertainment environment, designing the Circus Room of the Fairmont Hotel, the Top of

the Mark, the Patent Leather Lounge at the St. Francis Hotel, and the Bal Tabarin (now Bimbo's) on Columbus Avenue.

Pflueger was a pioneer rather than an imitator. His San Francisco office-towers brought him national recognition (the Pacific Telephone Building in 1925 and the Medical-Dental Building at 450 Sutter Street in 1930), and he came to the design of the Paramount at the height of his reputation and powers—and at a time when an entirely new style of design was evolving. This was Art Deco (both the phrase and the trend referred to the 1925 *Exposition des Arts Decoratifs et Industriels* in Paris), or Moderne as it was alternatively called: a streamlining and simplification of the elaborateness of Art Nouveau; an exhilarating use of new technologies and sciences; an electrifying interest in vibrant coloring and the effect of unity of detail.

The style, in all its glorious eclecticism and bracing simplicity of line, could almost have been designed for the man, and Pflueger seems to have greeted it just that way. For the Paramount, he worked with a staff of talented artists and draftsmen

Two bands and several orchestras turned out for the groundbreaking, as did the mayors of ten East Bay cities; and the ceremonies at Hobart (now 21st Street) and Broadway were followed by a parade. The Paramount's 38-year-old architect, Timothy Pflueger (above), was also on hand, and would cross the bay by ferry many times in the year ahead, for the San Francisco Bay Bridge which he would later help to design had not yet been built. The son of German immigrants, Pflueger had endured a hardworking childhood, taking his first job at the age of eleven, apprenticing himself to an architectural firm at sixteen and working his way up to a full partnership. He later became a founder of San Francisco's Museum of Modern Art and president of the San Francisco Art Institute. When he died in 1946, having suffered a heart attack on the way to his car one evening, the San Francisco Examiner *observed that thousands had known him as "Tim Pflueger, the rumpled, stocky, cheerful man who looked far more like a retired football fullback than his city's leading architect," and said that he had died "as he had lived for many years—on the streets of his beloved city and well within the sight of half a dozen towering buildings that bore his inimitable trademark."*

to design a building whose austerely functional exterior is a perfect foil for what it cloaks: a soaring double stairway, a billowing "Fountain of Light," a wealth of artistic detail on walls of silver and gold leaf, an amazing and enduring tribute to the world of the imagination.

Part of Pflueger's genius lay in his uninhibited energy, and this went hand in hand with an unreserved appreciation of life. His work was not an escape from the mundane so much as a celebration of it: his buildings were designed to place both new scientific developments and new artistic techniques at the service of ordinary human comfort and enjoyment. Far from scorning the ways of industry, he was a great respecter and serious student of these ways, interested in the technologies and needs—including commercial needs—of each enterprise for which he created a design. His early notes for the Paramount addressed the mechanics of the motion-picture business and stipulated a projection booth that would be "complete with synchronous room, rewind room, battery room, rheostat room, generator room, etc." Concerned with sight-lines, he designed a balcony that was suspended from the two side walls by means of a single steel girder so large and heavy (105 tons) that it had to be rolled to the construction site on logs. Concerned with sound, he built an acoustical model for the auditorium, designed textured side walls, and used perforated fabric on the rear wall—a forerunner of acoustical tile.

The problems of attracting moviegoers interested him, too. The curving lines of the sidewalk beneath the marquee (which are no longer there) were meant, he explained, to "urge the pedestrian intending to pass to turn and enter." And instead of subordinating advertising to 'art' in designing the theater's exterior, he created a vertical neon sign that rose 120 feet above the sidewalk and could be

PARAMOUNT THEATRE

seen throughout most of Oakland. "The Sign and Marquee," he assured the editor of the newsletter *Signs of the Times*, "were designed by the Architects, as an integral part of the building."

This letter-to-the-editor was one of many, for Pflueger shared with another great architect of his day, Frank Lloyd Wright, both a flair for showmanship and the perfect unselfconsciousness that often accompanies genius. Not only did he embrace the world of commerce, he unabashedly courted it in the promotion of the Paramount, orchestrating a publicity campaign, providing captioned photographs for magazines and newspapers, and promising exclusive material to editors. "Tell about the perfect acoustics," he urged the theater chain's public relations staff. "Why not tell, in a delicate manner, about those novel ceilings . . . .? These appointments and their decoration should be played up. No house in the Bay District, and perhaps the West Coast, equals it."

There may have been a touch of urgency to this particular campaign—"Don't forget," he added, "that in the whole theatre an effort has been made to give the public something to enjoy, and the publicity men something to talk about"—for the Depression had worsened steadily throughout the Paramount's construction. Indeed, financial problems had left Publix Theatres unable to complete the theater, and it had been sold, while still under construction, to Fox-West Coast Theatres. The construction and entertainment industries were both hard-hit by the Depression, and Milton Pflueger—who joined his brother's firm just a half-year before the stock market crash of October 1929—remembers the long list of draftsmen who left the firm early in the new decade because there was no work.

Yet as the economic situation hardened, so did the determined optimism and good cheer. "Adding greater beauty and splendor to our city," trumpeted the *Oakland Tribune* as if announcing a prizefight contender, "standing as a magnificent tribute to its architects and builders, Oakland's new $3,000,000 Paramount Theatre will throw open its doors tomorrow night at 5." The gala opening took place on December 16, 1931—a year and four days after the groundbreaking—and the lines began forming hours ahead of time for the first-come first-served tickets (sixty cents for a balcony seat and eighty-five cents for a seat in the orchestra or loge). By the time the early winter darkness fell and five o'clock arrived, Broadway was thronged with eager fans.

A platform had been erected in front of the Paramount, and the visiting stars of the silver screen—George Bancroft, Elissa Landi, John Boles, Francis Dee, and John Breedon, all of whom had arrived that morning aboard the Southern Pacific 'Owl' after an all-night Pullman-car trip from Hollywood—appeared on this platform first, for the benefit of spectators who had not arrived early enough to obtain a ticket. Even though it had the second largest auditorium in the West, the Paramount could not accommodate a crowd of this size, but loudspeakers broadcast the opening ceremonies taking place onstage to those outside. California's governor, "Sunny Jim" Rolph, introduced by Oakland mayor Fred Morcom, gave a brief speech. The theater was dedicated "to the service of the community," and the visiting luminaries from the twin empyrean realms of politics and show business were introduced. And then it was time for the show.

Those who were fortunate enough to have gotten inside saw a feature film ("The False Madonna," starring Kay Francis), a Fox Movietone newsreel, and a Silly Symphony animated cartoon ("The Spider and the Fly"), and heard the music of the Paramount's own orchestra, under the direction of Lew Kosloff.

Last on the program was that fleeting movie-palace phenomenon, a legacy from the vaudeville of the twenties: the stage show—in this case Fanchon & Marco's "Slavique Idea," a forty-minute revue featuring Sam Hearn, comedians Brock and Thompson, dancer LaVonne Sweet, the acrobatic Seven Arconis, Patsy Marr, and the Sunkist Beauties in a rousing chorus-line finale.

It should have been a dazzling display of the new theater and of the entertainment arts it had been built to showcase. But "The False Madonna" was disappointing and the reviews of the gala premiere were subdued. Perhaps even then there was something in the air; within six months the Paramount would close its doors, unable to meet operating expenses of more than $27,000 per week. Competing with the Paramount was the neighboring Fox-Oakland Theater, which had opened in 1928. Fox-West Coast had handed the management of its ailing chain of theaters to the Skouras brothers, well-known East Coast theater entrepreneurs, and had given them carte blanche; and the brothers had decided to eliminate competition within the ranks. The Paramount stayed closed for nearly a year, and when it reopened, the hoopla was gone, the orchestra pit and dressing rooms were empty, the stage crew had vanished. The Paramount had settled down to being just a movie theater.

Photograph by Gabriel Moulin

The underside (or soffit) of the Paramount's rectangular marquee was studded with 2,860 15-watt bulbs. Beneath it, the polished black granite walls and black-lacquered doors, with their chrome trim, are a study in black and silver. The chromium-plated discs inset in the walls, bas reliefs of wildlife by Theodore Bernardi, provide a key to the motifs of the interior decor. The Paramount still greets you in just this way.

But what a movie theater! What critics and reporters were invited to tour on the day before the opening—what eager theatergoers saw on opening night—was an architectural achievement which alone would have won a lasting reputation for its designer, and on a scale that defied belief. There was more than a mile of neon tubing in the marquee and sign, and the two together, suspended above the sidewalk, weighed twenty tons. Inside the theater, nearly an acre of floor space awaited, clad in more than 3500 yards of carpeting. The ceiling of the Grand Lobby, over fifty feet high, was an extraordinary metallic filigree lit by hidden green lights to suggest the foliage of a rain forest. (It was also part of the ultra-modern air-conditioning system.) Rare and costly materials were everywhere: hand-adzed quartered oak, Hungarian ash crotch, birdseye maple, Balinese rosewood, Malaysian teak, Italian marble. The stage proscenium, at sixty-six feet, was wider than that of the San Francisco opera house (which opened the following year), and the stage rigging could accommodate thirty-nine separate backdrops.

Despite the massiveness of scale, no slightest fixture or obscurest corner had been produced by rote or left to chance. Each detail of the Paramount partakes of an overall theme in which Nature is celebrated in outlines that range from the classical Greek to the stylized, modish Moderne. Particular forms—the shape of a leaf, the arch of a fountain or rainbow, the sinuous curves of a vine—are echoed, now accurately, now geometrically, on all sides. Everything rewards the gaze, and yet, as is often remarked, the overall effect is of a great unity which transcends both its details and its era and makes the Paramount's design timeless. This unity of effect probably explains why the Paramount was hailed by the critics of the day as a work of genius, and why the passage of five decades has neither dimmed its luster nor altered the experts' appraisals.

Several aspects of Pflueger's method of operation were relevant to this. First was his passionate interest in and involvement with the world of art. Beginning with his first commercial structures, he made it part of his policy to hire artists to contribute to his buildings. This was less unusual for such monumental buildings as the Stock Exchange than it was for motion-picture palaces, where the art was more likely to be copied than original. The Rapp brothers, George and C.W., benefitted from the great influx of artisans into the Chicago area after World War I, and hired these artisans to do the elaborate plaster moldings that decorated their rococo imitations. But in commissioning such well-known San Francisco artists as Robert B. Howard and Charles Stafford Duncan for a theater, Pflueger was relatively unique.

In his methods of collaborating with such artists, he may have been even more unique, for he seems to have been capable of transmitting the fire of inspiration, so that his own ideas and visions sparked creativity instead of dousing it. Having commissioned Charles Stafford Duncan to create a mural for the Women's Smoking Room on the lower level, Pflueger proceeded to suggest the colors for it, including the room's predominant and startling black. Another example of his involvement at this level is the sculpted wall panels which are a significant factor in both the acoustics and esthetics of the auditorium. These were drawn as part of the overall interior design of the building. But they were executed by Robert Howard, the son of architect John Galen Howard, who sculpted the molds for the plaster panels.

Photograph by Gabriel Moulin

Above the orchestra pit, a spectacular panel of sculpted plaster by Robert Howard and Ralph Stackpole shows Poseidon rising from the sea, and horses (his gift to man—including Pegasus, steed of the Muses) rearing on either side of him. The line of his outspread arms is continued in the sections of grillwork which take off from this sounding board; the waves of the sea are repeated in the waterfall ripples of the organ console. From another vantage point (above) the auditorium is a sea of flowers beneath a ceiling of stars. The modelled and sculpted walls diffuse the sound waves, and together with the modified megaphone shape of the room help account for its excellent acoustics.

23

Photograph by Gabriel Moulin

Pflueger also had artists on his staff, including draftsmen who could not only do the usual architectural tasks, but could in addition design mosaics, murals, and bas reliefs. Like a conductor with an orchestra of gifted and enthusiastic musicians, Pflueger inspired, led, and harmonized their efforts. For buildings like the Paramount, the master concept and the multitudinous details were outlined by him, worked on literally in concert in his office, and then executed and/or supervised by the indi-

vidual artists, to whom Pflueger made sure credit was given.

But the architect's interest in detail went well beyond the esthetic and into the practical. Pflueger was avidly interested in new developments, and consistently incorporated them in his work. Appropriately, the Paramount was the first building in Oakland to receive electricity through underground conduits rather than from power poles. This innovation on the part of the utility company was

Photograph by Gabriel Moulin

matched by the theater's up-to-date and even forward-looking wiring, heating, ventilating and cooling systems, and by the very last word in stage equipment and maintenance tools. At the Paramount, cleaning was to be facilitated by a central vacuuming system, with hoses plugged into hose outlets that were built into the baseboards in unobtrusive places, and with an enormous vacuum tank located in a basement room.

But it was in the theater's unique lighting design that the esthetic and the practical came together, in corner panels and recessed domes and jewel-like sconces, in fountains and columns and entire walls of light. Pflueger took full advantage of both the freedom and the functionalism of the Art Deco approach (which included the recognition of lighting engineering as a 'new science'), and used the newest materials—with, in those days of seemingly limitless supplies of power, no thought for energy conservation.

So naturally the lights were the first things to go, as the once-bright future of the movie palace dimmed. The Paramount went dark in June 1932, closing its doors just a half-year after opening them. The days when movie theaters could support not just the showing of movies, but entire orchestras and stage shows and platoons of uniformed attendants, were over just as the Paramount was being completed, and it had opened as an anachronism.

When it reopened in May 1933, it was under the management of Frank Burhans—originally the manager of the Warfield in San Francisco (where Fanchon & Marco had staged their first movie-house spectacular), and after that the manager of Fox-West Coast's Orpheum Theater in Oakland, where he won for himself the reputation of an effective troubleshooter. Mr. Burhans was commissioned to get the Paramount out of debt, and his method for achieving this was to operate without either a stage show or an orchestra, and to unscrew lightbulbs. "I'll grant," he said, reminiscing with *Oakland Tribune* critic Wood Soanes sixteen years later, "that the illumination got pretty dim and that some people suggested I should equip them with miners' lamps in order to find their way from the street to their seats, but we saved a lot of money."

Burhans' frugality was complemented by the policies of Fox-West Coast's new district manager, Richard Spier, who wisely eliminated the competition between the Paramount and the Fox-Oakland by sharing the best of the new motion pictures between them—including such features as "Dancing Lady" with Joan Crawford and Clark Gable, "Baby Take a Bow" starring Shirley Temple, "Dames" with Dick Powell and Ruby Keeler, and Fred Astaire and Ginger Rogers in "The Gay Divorcee."

Within less than a decade, the Depression gave way to the war years, and the port city of Oakland became a major departure-and-arrival point for servicemen. The city's hotels were constantly filled to capacity, and the Paramount's fortunately comfortable chairs and spacious lounges soon began serving as impromptu resting places for those in need of a roof over their heads. As the forties turned into the fifties, popcorn machines and candy counters were installed, and the incandescent lights in the Grand Lobby 'walls' were taken out and replaced by neon tubing in red and blue. Smoking was by then a ubiquitous activity; no room was exempt from tobacco fumes. Smoke coated the frosted glass lighting fixtures, dimming them even more than Manager Burhans had managed to, and ate its way into the once-magnificent curtain. The carpet succumbed gradually to years of constant foot-traffic; as it wore out, it was patched or replaced in areas, using nonmatching carpeting.

And still the Paramount struggled gallantly not just to stay afloat but to stay abreast of what was going on in the world. In 1953, it introduced CinemaScope to the East Bay with a showing of "The Robe." In 1957 Elvis Presley played in "Jailhouse Rock"—complete with an ensuing 'disturbance' in which a thousand young people milled around in the theater, an episode which the management downplayed.

By the time the decade of the fifties was drawing to a close, the ever vulnerable motion-picture industry was again under attack. This time it was losing patrons to television. The Paramount's management responded to the challenge with talent shows, prize nights, and cooperative advertising campaigns. Right to the end, the Paramount displayed an interest in the same thing its architect had been intrigued by: the 'very latest thing.' The last paid-attendance movie, shown on September 15, 1970, was the Beatles' film, "Let It Be."

And even this was not the end. The following year, the Paramount was included in the Historic American Buildings Survey, and photographs and documentation were placed on file in the Library of

Congress—the first formal, official recognition of its unique place in American architecture as one of the outstanding surviving Art Deco theaters in the United States.

At the end of that same year, 1971, a Warner Brothers movie, "The Candidate," was filmed, using the interior of the Paramount as one of the principal locations. And a local bank began rewarding its depositors with free monthly matinees at the Paramount.

Meanwhile, the Oakland Symphony Orchestra Association, looking for a new home for the orchestra and considering all possible alternatives to the expensive construction of a new symphony hall,

had begun to look at the Paramount. Several other cities—all of them in the East—had proven that the splendid old movie palaces could have splendid new uses; and sure enough, a feasibility study revealed some heartening surprises, including the theater's acoustics, which had of course originally been designed with an orchestra in mind. In October of 1972, the Paramount was purchased by the Oakland Symphony for one million dollars, half of which was donated by the seller, National General Theatres—the Old Fox-West Coast— with the other half coming from generous private donors. The theatre whose first period of glory had blazed so briefly now had bright new prospects.

Photograph by Gabriel Moulin

BACK FOR AN ENCORE:

The Restoration of the Paramount

In 1972 the Paramount's brilliant promise wasn't clearly visible to everyone who inspected the theater. True, the underlying structure was sound; the acoustics were excellent; the electrical system had been so modern and so well installed in 1931 that it was still up to code. But the dirt and damage that had accumulated in the interior during four decades of daily public use made it difficult to see what the Paramount had been and could again become. Where once each detail had been a delight, now it was more likely to be a source of dismay. From the garish neon of the Grand Lobby to the grime-coated walls of the auditorium, from the patched carpet to the scratched murals to the smudged Fifties candy counters in the foyer, it appeared at first that whatever was not stained, torn, or broken

was simply gone. Such grim disarray was an obstacle to the idea of restoring the Paramount, because many who saw the theater in this condition concluded that its interior would have to be completely redesigned.

Theirs was not an unusual outlook. Restoration and historic preservation were still relatively obscure concepts in the early seventies, and this was particularly true when it came to movie theaters, traditionally regarded as architecturally un-serious and not worth preserving, let alone restoring. Typically, San Francisco's fabulous Fox Theatre had been razed in 1963 to make way for a shopping-and-office-tower complex—a loss now considered inestimable. Nationwide, all of the very few movie palaces which had been taken over for use as concert halls (five in all, including Powell Hall in St. Louis and Heinz Hall in Pittsburgh) had been converted or renovated rather than restored.

An additional obstacle to the restoration of the Paramount was the fact that Art Deco had not yet been given the full measure of appreciation it later received as an architectural style. The idea of authentically restoring an Art Deco movie palace was, for these reasons and on the surface of it, highly improbable.

But the man whose idea it was a force to be reckoned with. Jack Bethards—sought out by Harry Lange, president of the Oakland Symphony Orchestra Association—came to the Paramount project with an unusual background. He had a degree in business administration, and broad experience in marketing and management consulting; but he had also been a professional musician, a stage-crew contractor, and the business manager of an opera company. Equally significantly, he had a long-standing interest in old theaters and had even made a tour of them ten years earlier, visiting the famous New York Roxy the day before it succumbed to the wrecking ball. And Bethards' favorite architectural style was, as it happened, Art Deco. Invited to leave the San Francisco Opera to become executive director of the Oakland Symphony, he agreed—provided he be given the direction, also, of the Paramount's fate.

But the task he confronted was, as he knew, enormous. In addition to the obvious needs of the interior, there were also the theater's main systems to consider: lighting, heating, air conditioning, stage rigging, sound and communication. To direct the work of restoration, Bethards turned to Peter Botto, also on the San Francisco Opera's business staff, whose background was remarkably similar to Bethards' in its combination of theatrical and business interests. Botto, a San Franciscan, had begun his career facing the footlights, and had then moved into house and box-office management. He headed the Theater Guild's subscription depart-

They may have feet of clay, but their heads are in the stars. The figures that flank the Paramount's towering neon sign are deities of the new art, Cinema—puppeteers, offering the world an unprecedented variety of amusements. The mosaic, designed by architect Timothy Pflueger and artist Gerald Fitzgerald, was blown up to its full size in the Foster & Kleiser billboard plant. Each tile was then delineated, colored, and numbered. The resulting full-size template was used by the Gladding-McBean Tile Company to execute the finished mosaic. All of the main motifs of the Paramount's interior appear here, and there are seventy colors in all—some of them, Pflueger noted, quite hard to achieve in tile.

ment in New York before accepting a position as ticket sales manager for the opera. But he had no prior experience in architectural restoration, and he resisted Bethards' offer of the challenging job until he saw the theater. The theater, he says, was irresistible. He immediately began assembling a team of dedicated experts: artisans and craftsmen who would work, as their earlier counterparts obviously had, for the sheer love of the work and the building.

They would have to work quickly and efficiently, for despite the dedicated work of civic-minded fund raisers led by Joe and Dee Knowland, funds were limited. It would later be pointed out that one of the many remarkable aspects of the theater's restoration is that it was not funded by taxpayers; another is that it was accomplished within the one-million-dollar limit of its budget. "Please compare that," invites theater historian Steven Levin, "to the 1970 estimate of $15 to $20 million to build a new hall." Even more arresting is the comparison with the $30 million or more it was estimated it would take to replace the Paramount as it is.

A second reason for haste was that the Oakland Symphony, confronted with declining ticket sales, was badly in need of a new home. The restored Paramount would be a glittering showcase: just the thing, Bethards felt, to spark renewed community interest in the symphony. The deadline was set: the Paramount would have to be ready for the opening of the orchestra's new season in September. There would be nine months in which to accomplish an authentic restoration of the theater.

'Authentic' is a key word; the replacement, duplication, and even re-invention of fifty-year-old artifacts and techniques was a colossal undertaking, made more complicated by the fact that Art Deco or Moderne design enjoyed the briefest of reigns, and, crushed between the flapper era and the Great Depression, left no generous legacy of materials. But on the subject of authenticity, Bethards and Botto were firm. They regarded Timothy Pflueger's Paramount as a work of art that could not be improved upon. "Everything," says Bethards, "took second place to that. Every time a decision arose that was 'practical utility' versus 'artistic integrity,' we always leaned toward the artistic integrity of the building. Pflueger's work came above everything."

To ensure that the restoration would be faithful to Pflueger's original conception, they hired San Francisco historian Steven Levin, President of the Theatre Historical Society, and he began at once to sift through historical records and archives in search of the original Paramount. His work was greatly aided by the fact that the Pflueger architectural firm (Miller & Pflueger at the time of the theater's construction, Milton T. Pflueger at the time of the restoration)—San Francisco's oldest continuously family-owned architectural firm—still had all of its records, drawings, and photographs of the 1931 building, and made all of them available.

Botto, meanwhile, pursuing authenticity, sought out Anthony Heinsbergen, painter and decorator of interiors for more than seven hundred theaters. Heinsbergen had wanted to do the Paramount's interior when the theater was being built, but had been the highest bidder for the job. He emerged from retirement at the age of 78 when opportunity knocked a second time.

Work began on the morning of December 20, 1972, after the last of the monthly matinees had taken place the day before (a film called, appropriately, "Joy in the Morning"), with the old mohair seats being taken up first, and then the carpeting. As the Paramount was stripped down, everything that might conceivably be of value to someone else was stashed in the lobby: popcorn makers and buttering machines, glass-fronted cases and candy vending machines. Buyers were sought, and payments were poured back into the massive restoration project. The carpeting was sold to a

Above the Paramount's main entrance, scallops of sandblasted, etched glass billow and foam and erupt in a Fountain of Light. Angle irons hold the glass panels in place and amber lights illuminate them at sharp angles, bringing out the lines of the design. Architect B. J. S. Cahill called this the "Fountain of Life," and pointed out that it contains hints of the life-forms that are found throughout the theater; a close look reveals fish shapes in its waves. Cahill also looked at the fountain from a distance and thought he saw a seated Buddha. Pflueger disagreed; but once you have seen the seated Buddha it is hard to make him go away. The view on the previous page shows why Pflueger said that the Paramount's Grand Lobby had "no solid wall and no solid ceiling." All is light and glass; illusion and illumination.

highway contractor, who would use it to season new paving. The seats too were bought, by a supplier who reupholstered them and sold them to other Bay Area theaters.

After the Paramount had been cleared, scaffolding was erected in the auditorium and in the Grand Lobby, lending a cathedral-like appearance to these cavernous spaces. Next, an unusual technique was employed: workmen wearing masks and carrying compressed-air hoses did a sort of reverse-vacuuming of the theater, literally blowing the dirt out. Peter Botto explains: "I didn't want to have the auditorium cleaned and have all the space *around* the auditorium still dirty, because with the air always moving through the air-conditioning system, the place would get dirty again. So we started way up at the top, in the attic, and blew everything down and out. The theater was probably cleaner when we reopened it than it had been in 1931—because we found that a lot of the original construction debris was still there."

Next came the washing of the many begrimed walls, a delicate task because of the varying kinds of surfaces—plaster, metal, glass, wood veneer, gold leaf, painted canvas—some of which could have been ruined by the use of the wrong cleaning material. The painters did much of this work by hand, cautiously testing both cleaning and finishing solutions. The walls had to be washed from bottom to top instead of the other way around, because when grimy water rolled down from above, its grit became embedded in the dirt already there. Meanwhile, the water cascading down the walls and pouring from the balcony onto the concrete floor was vacuumed up with giant construction vacs.

And while all of this was going on, another kind of work went ahead behind the scenes: the painstaking work of replacement. Luckily, pieces of the elaborately patterned old carpet were found in the uppermost balcony. These were taken to the original weaver, the Alexander Smith Carpet Company, who arranged for a replica to be woven in their mills in Greenville, Mississippi. Many of the original dyes were no longer available, and had to be duplicated by a complex system of mixing and matching which was aided by computer analysis. Also, it was no longer feasible to manufacture the carpet in twenty-seven-inch widths; this time it was done in nine-foot widths, with some nylon added to the formerly all-wool formula to facilitate cleaning and increase durability. The result was a near-perfect replication of the Art Deco carpeting, in all its exotic hues and with its pattern of volutes and stylized natural shapes carefully reproduced.

The seats were the next challenge. The Paramount's restoration team had learned that the high-pile mohair with which the original seats were

With its tropical yellows and greens, the Grand Lobby has the ambience of a rain forest. The leafy pattern of its ceiling is created by a grillwork of galvanized metal strips riveted together and suspended edgewise by steel cables. Hidden green lights placed alongside this grillwork shine upward against a white plaster reflecting surface, and the light is filtered through the gracefully patterned metal as it might be through forest leaves. But the grillwork is not merely decorative; through it blow the refreshing breezes of the Paramount's conditioned air. Opposite the Fountain of Light, the metallic curtain of foliage— punctuated by an oval window—descends to provide an elegant entrance to the mezzanine at the top of a double stairway.

The golden maidens who beckon you in toward the foyer are purely decorative, and stand amidst the fountains whose lines echo the Fountain of Light and the arcs of the carpet. Their skirts are vaguely Polynesian, their angular poses faintly Egyptian, their streamlined faces startlingly modern. They set the tone of the strange, the mysterious, the faraway. The carpet (right) was painstakingly reproduced by the original weaver when the theater was restored. Its unusual pattern bears the motifs of leaf, vine and flower which are repeated throughout the theater; its fern shapes prefigure the volutes of the organ grill.

covered was now very expensive and very rare. Only one firm in the United States even manufactured it—Piedmont Plush Mills of Greenville, South Carolina. The Paramount's order amounted to most of a year's production for this small factory, yet it had to be produced in well under a year, shipped to San Francisco to have its stenciled pattern dyed, and forwarded from there to American Seating in Grand Rapids, Michigan.

The seats themselves, the best available, would be roughly two inches wider than the originals, to accommodate the broadened girth of the average American and to provide the kind of comfort which audiences have come to expect—which also meant thicker seat-backs, and cushions with serpentine springs instead of the old-style coils. However, the original decorative end-standards would still be used.

Among the most unexpected challenges were the main stage curtain and valance, which, like the lighting, had been designed by Michael Goodman. A drapery cleaning firm had been called in to perform the demanding task of cleaning and re-appliqué which would obviously be necessary; but it was discovered that beneath the old appliqué lurked hints of the curtain's former true color, an astonishing bright rust which had, in forty smoke-filled years, turned a uniform dull brown. Tests confirmed that this original color could never be recaptured through cleaning; the entire curtain and valance would have to be recreated.

For this task, the restorers turned to Marvin and Kay Burkman, experts in theatrical draperies. The Burkmans covered the floor of the stage with the old curtain and valance and meticulously traced the patterns and outlines onto craft paper. Seams and hems were torn out to find fabric samples that had not been exposed to air, and fabrics were dyed to match these samples. Working at home in San

Francisco over a period of five months, in a garage that had been converted into a drapery factory, the Burkmans appliquéd ornate patterns of silver and gold lamé and hammered satin onto velour in a detail-perfect replication which incorporated even an inconsistency in the design of the original curtain. By the time they were finished, they had stitched their way through more than 1700 yards—nearly a mile—of fabric.

Meanwhile, back at the theater, painters had established their headquarters in the Women's Restroom and Cosmetic Room on the lower floor, and had begun their main task. Two brothers from the Heinsbergen studio in Los Angeles, Frank and Tom Bouman, commuted to Oakland each week to supervise the painting and train the painters in the art of 'leafing,' a process which is thought to have originated in Egypt in the fourteenth century B.C. The Egyptians worked with paper-thin sheets of real gold, which is prohibitively expensive and has never been used in the theater; instead, leafing was done with Dutch Metal ("fake" gold leaf, an alloy), aluminum leaf (in place of silver), and variegated leaf (another alloy, containing some copper). Many of the columns, bas reliefs, doorframes, statues, and light fixtures received this leafing

treatment. The golden maidens of the Grand Lobby required at least 120 leaves each.

The painters had other interesting challenges as well. The walls of the two Men's Lounges were veneered with precious woods: quartered oak on the lower floor and ash crotch (which has a watered-silk pattern) on the mezzanine. These wood veneers were too thin to be refinished; they had to be delicately cleaned and then lacquered numerous times. In the process of working on the walls of the mezzanine-level lounge, the painters became curious about the metallic-looking sign above the Men's Room door. Someone had noticed that it was the only painted sign in the theater, and it proved to be merely cardboard. Cautiously removing it, they were astonished to find an incised design behind it: the gammadion, a mystic and religious symbol which had been used throughout recorded history. Shortly after the Paramount was built, the gammadion had been tipped on its edge by the Nazis and turned into the world's most hated sign; it had apparently been discreetly covered, at the Paramount, ever since. After much discussion, the restoration team decided to adhere to Pflueger's original design, and the cardboard sign was permanently retired.

This intriguing anachronism, located atop the stairs to the mezzanine foyer, is a seat annunciator, part of the 'Tele-Chec' system, a standard feature of Paramount theaters which enabled the theater's staff to keep track of seating availability. Ushers stationed at the head of each aisle dialed the number of available seats in their sections on a dial inset in the wall. The numbers dialed were transmitted via telephone lines to the ornate seat annunciators in the foyers, and lighted corresponding numbers behind the vertical glass panels. The usher stationed in the center of each foyer—who was called a 'splitter'—could then greet entering customers with news of exactly where they might find seats: "There are three seats on Aisle Five, to your left, Madam." 'Sir' and 'Madam' were requisite forms of address in the halcyon days of ushering. Ushers were taught speech and deportment, theater-management skills, and even military maneuvers. At the Roxy Theater in New York they reported for work in battalions and were trained by a retired marine colonel.

There are sixty recessed panels (or coffers) in the vaulted ceiling of the mezzanine lounge, their gold and silver designs glazed, said the architect, "in lavender alternating tones going toward the red and toward the green." The room's mirror has frosted glass panels at its base to echo the Fountain of Light, whose reflection is caught in this photograph. On the doorframes, in silver leaf, a top-hatted gent and his gracefully gowned lady are surmounted by peacocks—symbols of beauty, immortality... and pride.

It has been estimated that an amazing sixty-five percent of the theater's original furnishings were still on the premises. Gone were the back-to-back sofas of the lower lounge, the small statues that had graced the tables, and the framed paintings and mirrors that had lined the foyers. Concentrating on the much that was left, administrators called in specialists to refinish the wood and reupholster the fabric areas, and they achieved striking resemblances to the originals.

Listed among the missing were four of the seven small chairs of the mezzanine Women's Cosmetic Room: delicate, armless period pieces. They looked impossible to duplicate, but a San Francisco firm (Pacific Woodworking) succeeded in matching them so closely that only a trained eye can discern which are duplicates and which originals.

However, the restoration effort did not always proceed smoothly.

Project manager Peter Botto, who had been working twenty-hour days, suffered a broken leg and had to direct the restoration from a hospital bed for a week. An entire roll of the mohair fabric for the auditorium seat-backs was printed upside-down and had to be returned. Jack Bethards, meanwhile, was meeting a different kind of obstacle as questions continued to arise about the advisability or necessity of authentic restoration. Shouldn't the name of the theater be changed? What about painting the walls white? One vision favored pagoda-shaped telephone booths on the mezzanine level. Another called for the removal of all the theater's colored lighting. But nonpartisan architectural and design consultants bore Bethards out, and the idea of authenticity carried the day.

Yet, paradoxically, the Paramount's new role as a fully professional arts theater would require certain subtle changes. The most significant departure

(continued on page 52)

A vine-and-flower-covered trellis in silver leaf frames the door of the mezzanine-level Women's Lounge, and stencilled, stylized fleurs-de-lys in the room's corners accentuate the suggestion of an arbor. In the Cosmetic Room, a true optical illusion: what appears to be wallpaper is really an elaborate mural in which Moorish castles are adrift behind cloud-like mountains in a palmy paradise. Also in the mural, if one looks closely, are the mask of Drama and the pipes and lyre of Music. Beyond the Cosmetic Room, through the door, the tiles of the restroom, in shades of lavender, echo the lavender glaze of the lounge ceiling.

In the design of the Paramount, the furniture is as exotic as the decor. On an ebony-based table with a marble top, colorful enamelled flowers nestle in such out-of-the-way places that they are seldom seen; but the statue of Diana is the center of attention here. The pattern of these enamelled flowers is precisely reproduced in the metallic ends of the sofas, whose 'tabletops' are veneered with Balinese rosewood in a radiating sunburst design. Attention to detail extended even to the air vents. This one (left) has a tropical look, but others have zigzag patterns, floral designs, musical notes. The 'jade' of the small side-table is painted tile.

In 1931 few women smoked in public, so an elegant private room was created on the lower level, adjoining the Women's Lounge. "Look up Ladies Smoking Room," Pflueger instructed himself in his diary in April 1931, "to see if opportunity for painting on wall by Dunc." 'Dunc' was prominent San Francisco artist Charles Stafford Duncan, whose murals have become one of the Paramount's most famous features. Lacquering was a fashionable Art Deco technique, and lacquered walls were the very last word in interior decor. "Duncan to call me," Pflueger wrote in July. "Suggest to him that he use black background . . .with gold, vermillion, greens, blues and white—some limited use of colors." The suggestion was well taken; what might be benign against a bright background becomes darkly elusive against a sea of black.

from the original design was the addition of a box office. Because tickets would most often be sold on a reserved-seat basis, the tiny showcase-style ticket booth in front of the theater would not be adequate. The architectural firm of Skidmore, Owings & Merrill designed a box office for the 21st Street side of the theater which would not alter the lines of the fine Broadway facade and would only slightly alter the side-door entrance, where the line of black-lacquer-and-etched-glass doors would be moved in toward the foyer. In the groundbreaking for this new box office, the gold-plated shovel used in the theater's original groundbreaking saw service again.

Another significant change was the addition of bars in the two general lounges (lower floor and mezzanine). These were also a nod in the direction

of the Paramount's new and more sophisticated role in Oakland's entertainment life, but they were designed as replicas of the orchestra rail in the auditorium, built of the same sober dark walnut, and varnished to the same dark sheen.

In the auditorium itself, the new seat widths mandated a shift in the location of the two intermediate aisles (numbers 2 and 4). The aisles of the Paramount are indented in the concrete of the floors, so that carpeted and uncarpeted areas will blend and present a smooth surface. Consequently the old aisles had to be filled in, and the new ones carved out, prior to the laying of the carpet. At the same time, the distance between rows was increased to provide more leg room, and space was created for wheelchairs and standees by omitting the last two

The men's lounges of the Paramount, with their veneered walls and terrazzo floors, are austere; but their austerity shows off the streamlined modernity of the Art Deco style. Note the two mirrors in the lower-level Men's Lounge. One of them is inset in the wall; the other masks a door which leads to the theater's service areas.

The view across the lower level's General Lounge, and into the Women's Lounge, shows one of the two bars added to the theater during the restoration. The red wall piers with their amber light panels recall the color scheme of the Grand Lobby. Framed by them in this photograph, above a couch whose upholstery very nearly reproduces the pattern of the carpet, Artemis—goddess of the moon and of wild animals—fills the sky with music, while the spark struck by her ram's hoof becomes a shooting star. This famous silver-leafed bas relief has become the logo of the Oakland Symphony. Above it is one of the Paramount's spectacular lighting fixtures, its reflectivity enhanced by the use of gold leaf.

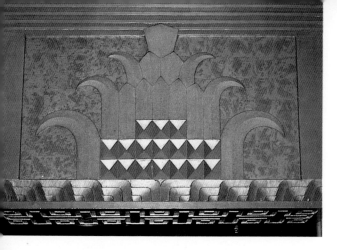

rows of seats and placing high rails for standees in the center and low rails for wheelchairs on either side of these. Altogether, these changes in seat width and placement reduced the theater's seating capacity from an original 3,476 to the present 2,998.

But these were just the changes that showed. Backstage, behind the scenes, and even under the ground, work was going on. The elaborate lighting system of the auditorium, which had been almost completely dismantled, was rewired and reconditioned. Additional electrical service was installed to increase the lighting possibilities the Paramount could offer to touring shows. The counterweight system—the epitome of stage design at the time the Paramount was built—was retained and reconditioned. The stage footlights, however, were removed so that when the orchestra pit is raised it creates a large and continuous stage floor. And an air filtration system was added along with the new air-conditioning equipment, replacing the old "air cleaning" system in which the air was passed through a chamber and sprayed with water vapor to "wash" it.

The lines of the main-floor foyer curve gracefully toward the 21st Street entrance, where an enlarged vestibule houses the Paramount's new box office. On the right, beneath the lighted sign, stairs lead down to the lounge areas of the lower level. On the left, gilded parrots crown one of the entrance doors to the auditorium, continuing the tropical-paradise theme of the decor. Just to the left of this door is one of the original seat-annunciator stations, through which ushers kept track of seating availability. The frosted glass panes of the main entrance and auditorium doors repeat part of the trellis pattern of the doorframes in the mezzanine-level Women's Lounge. Notice the gilded bas-relief ceiling borders.

From the Grand Lobby, this oval window seemed to be ensconced in an airy curtain of greenery (see page 37), but its setting in the foyer of the upper mezzanine is a solid wall, into which it is cut in jewel-like scallops. Through it, one has an excellent view of the Fountain of Light, which has been compared to a rose window because of its position in the theater; like the rose window of a cathedral, the fountain is above the entrance and isn't seen until one leaves—unless one seeks out a view such as this one.

Time passed, the margin narrowed; the theater swarmed day and night with activity as the night of the reopening approached. Marquee letters in the style of the sheet-metal-and-milk-glass originals were acquired; restroom signs duplicating the old ones were found or made. Work continued right down to the wire, and on the evening of the reopening itself—September 22, 1973—the last pieces of the valance were hung in place. The curtain was at last going up on the new old Paramount.

And in the best theater tradition, there was an ironic and unexpected hitch: the cables jammed, preventing the valance from being raised into position. When the theater opened precisely at seven o'clock, the doors to the auditorium were kept closed while stagehands clambered up to free it.

Outside, meanwhile, the public was being treated to another grand theater tradition: opening night. Searchlight beams struck into the sky and criss-crossed above red carpets; bands played; parking-lot attendants were clad in tuxedos. Everything was being done in the style of the old Paramount, and all who walked through the elegant black-lacquered doors saw what that style was. The program for this second gala opening in the theater's history had been planned as something-for-everyone night, but the concensus among critics was that the real show had been in front of the stage rather than on it. "Move over, Circus Maximus," said the *Berkeley Gazette*, "the Paramount is playing again."

Haven't I seen you somewhere before? The many bas reliefs that grace the Paramount's walls are of cast plaster, decorated with paint and gold leaf. The foreground pair in this view (right) of the mezzanine foyer were cast from the same molds as those that appear on the stairway (above) which leads from the mezzanine up toward the upper mezzanine and down toward the main-floor foyer. This stairway shows the elegantly simple lines which have made the theater's beauty classic and timeless.

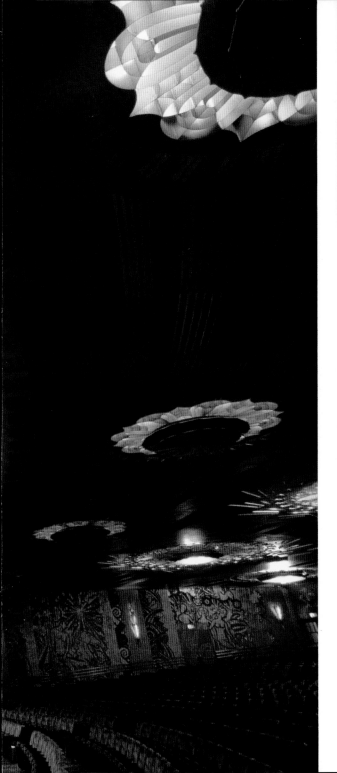

63

The 55-foot-high proscenium columns on either side of the stage look like frosted glass. In fact they are made of aluminum alloy which has been extruded in scalloped sections. The sections are assembled so that they overlap slightly and have small spaces between them, and columns of 75-watt lamps run up the inside, projecting light which shines through the columnar spaces. This was one of the two features of the Paramount so unique that Pflueger patented them. (The other was the auditorium ceiling.) The lighting instruments in front of the organ grill are hung from 'box booms,' so called because of their location, which in many theaters is the place where box seats are located. Above them is the side of the auditorium ceiling, which is studded with breastplates—light fixtures with a tortoiseshell look, which are really layers of concentric metal rings with clusters of colored lights between the layers. The balcony soffit's extraordinary light fixtures (right) have a lotus design. Lotuses, Egyptian water-lilies which opened at dawn and closed at sunset, became symbols of the sun in ancient mythology. Here, they double as vents for the theater's air-conditioning system.

Counseling the theater's public relations staff on how to introduce his revolutionary new ceilings to the press and public, Pflueger said, "If you wish to tell what it is, refer to it as silvery metal fins. Avoid the name of galvanized iron." Whether this was because he was in the process of obtaining a patent on his ceiling or because "galvanized iron" would destroy the lacy illusion is not known. But the tactic was effective. Bewildered reporters adopted his language, and the articles heralding the opening of the new theater are replete with allusions to those mysterious silvery fins. In the five sections of grillwork above the auditorium, enormous pyramidal leaves repeat the pattern of the stage valance, and Isis holds the sun aloft. Like Poseidon a fertility figure and symbol of regeneration, Isis was the Egyptian goddess of all life. Her legend tells of the sun overwhelmed by night and then reborn with the new day.

The Mighty Wurlitzer

In the days of the silent pictures, organs were considered not only standard, but essential to the large movie palaces: they both enlivened the films and (often) enlightened the audiences, providing musical cues to the action on the screen. These organs and their organists were so central to the entertainment that they were frequently advertised on the theater marquees. The biggest draw of all was the Hope-Jones Unit Orchestra, manufactured by the Rudolph Wurlitzer Company and known before long as the Mighty Wurlitzer.

By 1931, when the Paramount opened, the talkies had only been around for four years, and ideas about equipping a movie theater had changed very little—although they were about to change dramatically.

The Paramount's original organ was the seventeenth and last of a series of organs built by Wurlitzer for the Paramount Publix theaters: a four-manual, twenty-rank model called the Publix I, which cost $20,000 in 1931. It had a ripple-edged 'waterfall' console which was Wurlitzer's standard design for Art Deco theaters and which must have seemed particularly appropriate for the Paramount. This organ enjoyed a brief period of glory; but the theater closed in 1932, and reopened under relatively spartan conditions eleven months later, and after that the Wurlitzer was only used intermittently. In the late 1950s it was sold and put in storage, and after ten more years it was bought by a Los Altos, California, restaurant (Ken's Melody Inn). Another ten years went by, and the old Publix I (Opus 2164) was sold again: to the Paramount Music Palace restaurant in Indianapolis, where dedicated owners created an environment filled with memorabilia describing and depicting its original home.

The Paramount, meanwhile, underwent a long dry spell in the organ department. It was home, briefly, to a Rodgers electronic organ that used eighty speakers. Then even that was taken out.

When the restoration of the Paramount got under way, word was circulated among organ buffs that the theater was in need of an authentic movie-palace organ. A Los Angeles collector, J.B. Nethercutt, notified the Paramount's administrators that he had the very thing: the *first* Publix I (Opus 1123), which had started its career in Detroit's Capitol Theatre, and had gone from there to a skating rink and eventually into a collector's warehouse. It arrived at the Paramount in 1974. But it was incomplete and needed work.

Another Southern California collector, Preston Fleet, donated a major collection of Wurlitzer components. The Paramount's staff held an organ auction to sell parts from both donations that could not be used, and the resulting $40,000 was matched by a grant from the California Office of Historic Preservation. In the ensuing seven years, Opus 1123 was both restored and upgraded—to about the level of a Publix IV (the model installed in the Brooklyn Paramount and Boston Metropolitan theaters), with twenty-seven ranks of pipes and 213 stop keys. Its percussion division boasts a real vibraharp, piano, marimba harp and xylophone, and includes ten tuned percussions in all.

Architect Timothy Pflueger was particularly proud of the way the auditorium's side walls were "not interrupted by the usual heavily ornamented protruding organ front," and this absence of protrusion contributes to the auditorium's fine acoustics. The scrolled volutes of the grillwork, made of plaster cast in aluminum molds sculpted by Bay Area artist Robert Howard, conceal three organ chambers which contain the pipes and other instruments. The percussion shelf is above the main

chamber on the left side of the auditorium; and on the right side is the solo chamber. During the organ restoration, the main and solo chambers were reduced in area so that the sounds were projected outward, and their grill openings were refitted with the original wooden expression (or swell) shutters, which had been removed with the original organ. These shutters enable the organist to control the volume without limiting the number of effects used.

The Wurlitzer's wind system is powered by a 25-horsepower Spencer Orgoblo which was originally in San Francisco's historic California Theater.

Its electrical system, on the other hand, is from tomorrow rather than yesterday: a digital solid-state relay and switch system—one of the largest ever to be used for a pipe organ—through which impulses are transmitted from the organ console to all three chambers by means of a single coaxial cable. In another phase of the organ's restoration, the old screw-lift was replaced with a more modern hydraulic lift.

The Paramount Wurlitzer, in its new incarnation, made its debut in November of 1981, and is now an integral part of the theater's return to its original state.

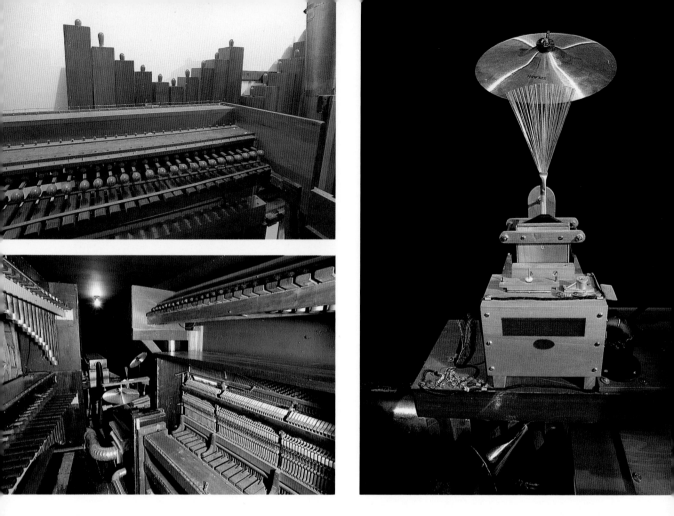

The organ's solo chamber (above left) is behind the grill on the right side of the auditorium. Here we see the small xylophone in the foreground, with the glockenspiel below it and the 'skyline' of the eight-foot tibia on top. The photograph below it shows the percussion shelf, which is on the left side of the auditorium, above the organ's main chamber. (In the photo at left on the preceding page, a light is on in the percussion shelf.) Not many people get this far behind the scenes; the percussion shelf is dizzyingly high up, and is reached by a vertical steel ladder. But the trip is rewarding when an organist is at the keyboard, because then these instruments appear to start playing by themselves, and make a ghostly music with no musician in sight. That's a marimba on the left, and a piano on the right, with the large xylophone above it. In the close-up of the jazz cymbal, an Acme siren can be seen below it—the 'whizz' in a 'whizz-bang'! We return to the solo chamber (far right) for a look at the brass ranks: trumpet and saxophone are shown here. Hidden away on the rear chest is the big booming tuba.

KEEPING IT GLOWING:

The Operation of the Paramount

Architect Timothy Pflueger designed a dazzling arena for the works of the human imagination, but he enveloped it in a solid network of utilities and support systems. Behind the golden walls, beneath the carpeted floor, and even above the lacy ceiling lurks an intriguing and seldom-glimpsed realm. It includes:

— a maze of underground passageways so extensive and confusing that 'road signs' must be posted at the corners;
— an electrical system so massive that the 'fuse box' is a room; and
— air ducts so large that a truck could be driven through them.

Those who work in a theater refer to it as a house, and the term offers an interesting perspective on what goes on at the Paramount, a house to which guests come by the thousands. The preparation for these guests requires such feats as the vacuuming or mopping of nearly an acre of floors and the dusting, waxing, scrubbing or polishing of everything on them. The checklist of items that must be kept spotless is a housekeeper's nightmare. Doors, windowpanes, wood furniture, lamps, water fountains, seats, mirrors, sinks, stair railings, telephone booths—all are made to shine in the glow of the soft lights.

The Paramount's architect created an edifice with entire walls and ceilings of light, in an era when energy was cheap. Now the theater's power costs thousands of dollars per month. For this reason, light use is held to an absolute minimum when the theater is not open to the public. 'Work lights' sparsely dot the huge dim expanses of the workaday Paramount, making miners' hats seem like a good idea and creating eerie interior landscapes.

But even when the lights are all brightly glowing, a visitor to the Paramount's public areas may have difficulty spotting a single lightbulb, because the lighting is almost entirely indirect. The fact that the lightbulbs are hidden makes some of them quite hard to reach; the theater's staff changes these regularly, utilizing (among other things) a custom made ladder with one leg shorter than the other (for use on steps) and built-in ladders concealed in some of the columns. The suspended circular fixtures of the auditorium are counterbalanced, and can be raised through the ceiling.

Also to be considered are the computer-controlled stage lights, the carbon-arc spotlights and projectors, backstage service and dressing-room area lights, emergency and work lights, and even the music-stand lights.

But the maintenance of the Paramount as a clean, well-lighted place is just the beginning of the management's concerns. In the theater's administrative offices, the many details of upkeep and repair are coordinated with the staggering thousands of other details involved in the running of a theater of this size; and the combination of the vast scale and the welter of minute particulars makes the job uniquely challenging. Among the items dealt with daily are:

— promotion and the booking of shows, and the coordination of the theater's rehearsal and performance schedule with major maintenance projects (such as carpet shampooing, concrete-floor painting, and stage-rigging repair);
— ticket sales and box-office activities;
— accounting, bookkeeping, and payroll; and
— the coordination of an event staff which includes box-office personnel, doormen, ushers, security guards, bartenders, stagehands, projectionists, custodians, and volunteers.

When an event is booked, contracts must be prepared and signed, tickets and insurance ordered, and theatrical equipment and staff needs determined and arranged: How many stagehands will be needed? Will projectionists be required? Information is exchanged regarding the theater's rules and regulations, the show's length, intermission time, merchandising and personnel lists.

A full-time box office is maintained at the Paramount to handle advance sales and season subscriptions, as the theater is home to both the Oakland Symphony and the Oakland Ballet. In addition, it houses the orchestra's extensive library (which occupies a salaried librarian and a staff of trained volunteers), and it is a National Historic Landmark offering public tours.

In the reflecting chamber above the auditorium's filigree ceiling, 150 lamps whose light is tinted by colored rondels create a landscape that is seldom seen. The lamps are on nine different circuits, and can be mixed, brightened, dimmed to create any effect from desert sunset to northern lights. Because each lamp throws off heat from its 500 watts, the sensation from above is much closer to the desert than to the north pole. Step outside the reflecting chamber and you are on a catwalk, peering at the forest of steel cables from which the solid portion of the auditorium ceiling is suspended. The slender line of red light in the center of the picture (above right) comes from one of the breastplates, whose counterweights hang from a metal loop in the photo below. A view from the top (far right) shows the inside of one of the glowing proscenium columns. The reflecting surface of its interior looks pink here because of the colored lights; its color is really off-white.

The Oakland Symphony no longer owns the Paramount, although it maintains its administrative offices in the building. Concurrent with the theater's restoration, the Orchestra launched a fund-raising effort to create an endowment which would ensure operating funds for it. In an eerie parallel to the Paramount's early Depression-era history, the financial climate changed and the effort failed. On October 1, 1975, the Orchestra gave the Paramount to the city of Oakland for one dollar—plus stipulated use of the theater for rehearsals and performances over a period of years, the value of which would eventually equal the Orchestra's initial investment.

The Paramount is managed by Paramount Theatre of the Arts, Incorporated, a nonprofit corporation which was established to administer the theater for the city. It operates at a deficit, with revenues equalling roughly 65 percent of expenses and the city funding the balance. But what price can be put on history, heritage, the legacy left by one era and treasured by another? The Paramount's owners (the citizens of Oakland) and administrators are well aware of their theater's inestimable value. For this reason, the restoration of the Paramount is in a sense an ongoing project. The replacement for the original organ was worked on for more than seven years. An effort is still being made to locate missing furniture and works of art. Over a period of years, the entire exterior has been waterproofed to protect it. And the management was zealous in pursuing and obtaining for the theater another kind of protection: the status of National Historic Landmark which it acquired in 1977. A great part of the present-day operation of the theater goes toward the preservation in it of every vestige of the past.

But a great part also goes toward making it what it was meant to be: a first-class showplace as well as a place for a show; a theater so fine that part of the evening's entertainment is the sheer pleasure of being there. The constant and even gruelling work that is required for the creation of such an elegantly smooth surface is analogous to the discipline and practice that lie behind any fine performance.

Thinking of becoming a stagehand? Try a trip to the top first, and see how you like these heights. In this view from the loading dock high over the stage floor, light from lamps on the concrete ceiling is filtered through the heavy cross-hatching of the gridiron and the steel cables, giving an underwater look to the red curtain on the left and the blue backdrop on the right, both of which are hung from pipes suspended over the stage. Between these, several empty pipes are visible; for a particular show, they might hold backdrops, set units, or lights. This area above the stage is called the fly loft. It must be high enough for backdrops to be lifted into it (or flown, in stage parlance), out of the audience's view. Far below—far, far below, as if at the bottom of a canyon—is the stage, all lit up.

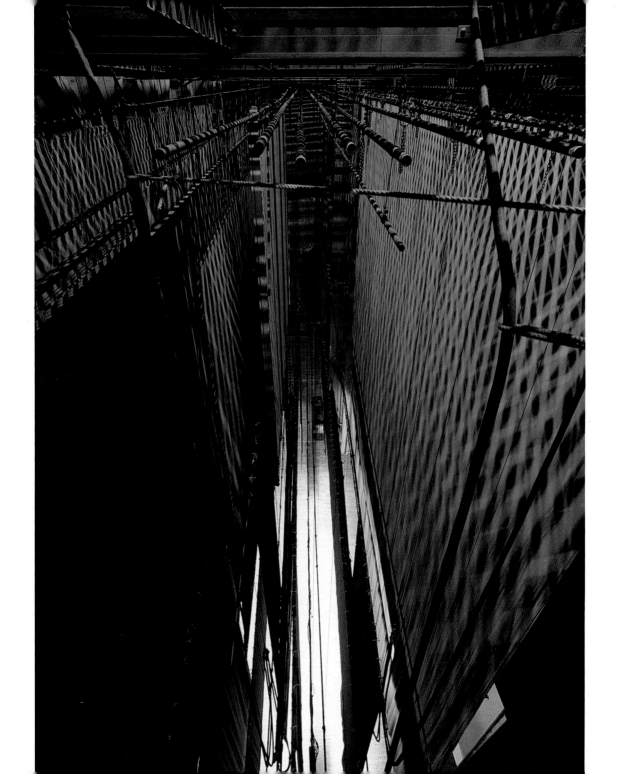

In this view (left) we have climbed several feet from the loading dock to the steel grid which forms a canopy 75 feet above the stage; and we have turned around, so that instead of facing the pipes and backdrops, we are looking at the lines of the counterweight system. There are 39 of these lines at the Paramount; for each of these, there are five steel cables, from which a pipe is suspended. At the other end of the cables, a counterweight container (called an arbor) holds iron weights which balance the weight of whatever is being hung from the pipe. If a curtain, for example, is to be hung, the pipe is lowered to within four feet of the stage. This raises the arbor to the level of the loading dock, where weights may be added to it. Sometimes a second or 'trailing' arbor must be added to balance a particularly heavy piece. The coiled ropes in the picture are drop-lines used for retrieving tools and equipment from the stage.

A Ballet Rehearsal

It is a Thursday afternoon, and a ballet company is rehearsing the next evening's performance. The Paramount's auditorium is dark and empty, and the dancers move around on the stage with an elegance of motion and intensity of concentration that contrasts oddly with their clothing: tee shirts and sweat suits, baggy shorts held up by suspenders, elephant-leg warmup socks. Backstage, a lighting engineer sits at a computer console, and occasionally a dance is interrupted, delayed, restarted to allow for adjustments in the lighting.

Despite the interruptions, the dancers maintain their concentration, which is punctuated now and then by a laugh, a gasp, a sneeze. Bathed in colored lights, clad in their casual attire, strictly formal in their movements, they resemble nothing so much as comical puppets; and this resemblance is amplified when, pirouetting into the wings, they slump briefly into wooden chairs, only to leap up again. Backstage, some of them dance, some stretch —bending over at the waist and dangling, again like puppets—and some watch the stage with great absorption. Several of the women point their toe shoes into a small pile of what looks like sand or ground glass: it is rosin, to keep the toes of the shoes from becoming slippery.

The stage is covered with a layer of hard black rubber which gives traction and flexibility. Prior to the performance it will be washed down with Ajax and water, because the dust that imperceptibly collects on its surface makes it slippery.

Behind the lighting engineer at his console, stagehands stand at the rail and work the lines which control the backdrops and curtains. And in the wings, trees of gelled lights create a jewelled effect whose brilliance temporarily blinds some of the dancers, so that, coming offstage, one of them gropes for a chair, saying, "Oooooh, I can't see a *thing*," and sits down dripping with perspiration. From the front of the auditorium, the director calls, "Again, please; I want to see that again."

In the photograph on the previous page, and again in the one on the right, we see the pin rail—a nautical term which reflects the fact that in the early days of English theater, much of the backstage work was done by sailors, who were familiar with ropes and rigging. Until the 1920s, all of a theater's rigging was accomplished with rope, to which sandbags were attached to counterbalance a load. (Many older theaters still operate this way; the ones that do are called 'hemp houses.') Now steel has replaced everything but the 'endless line': a circle of rope which is used to effect the raising and lowering. The levers along the pin rail are brakes, used to lock pipes in place at the desired height. In front of the Paramount's pin rail is a computer lighting console connected to dimmers housed in a room beneath the stage; a manual light-control switchboard; and, in the background, a patchboard which interconnects dimmers and lighting instruments.

Above we see the main curtain, tied back, and the house-lighting control board and patchboard. Next to the clock is a stop-clock, which is used to time intermissions, orchestral pieces, and anything in which split-second timing is a factor. The rope to the left of the main curtain is an endless line: pull on it one way and the curtain opens, pull on it the other way and the curtain closes. In a close-up, the light-control switchboard is set off against the red curtain. Each of the white keys is used to dim or brighten a particular set of lights. To the right of the switchboard is a corner of the computer console, and in the background, a thirty-foot extension ladder which is mounted on wheels. A stagehand climbs to the top to focus lighting instruments, while others steady and position the ladder.

A Travelling Show Arrives

It is one of Broadway's hit musicals, and tonight it will open at the Paramount. Precisely at eight A.M. its travelling crew, met by the Paramount's stage crew, begins to unload the large trucks that have pulled up outside the theater. From these trucks come a computer console and racks of dimmers for the show's own lighting system; a sound-system control console, stacks of speakers, and coils of cables; and even a washer and dryer for the wardrobe department—plus, of course, the scenery and props for the play.

The theater, which yesterday was dim and silent, now hums and swarms with people. Thick electrical cables are uncoiled and drawn up the side aisles, and lights are affixed to the balcony rail. Onstage, sets are assembled and backdrops hung, with crew members working in a cherrypicker and on ladders that extend thirty feet upward. "Pit going down," someone calls, and the orchestra pit descends, bearing a load of drums and a drummer who looks suddenly disconcerted. "Hey," he calls, "will this thing stop by itself?"

Prop locations are marked on the stage floor with black tape, and in the auditorium the sound system console has been set up; now an engineer wearing headphones leans over it, and music begins to play at various volumes, increasing the general level of noise.

All day, engineers and stagehands work intently and almost nonstop. When they are finished, at six o'clock, each smallest prop is in its place on the prop shelves backstage, and the theater is once again quiet and dark—but expectantly so. It is almost time for members of the troupe to start arriving.

The property man is the first to appear, and moves across the stage pushing a bucket on wheels with his mop handle, a classic and strangely familiar figure. Downstairs in the musicians' lounge the members of the orchestra are warming up.

Meanwhile, upstairs the doormen are slipping into their uniform jackets, the house manager into his tuxedo. Ushers arrive and are assigned to a head usher who will give them instructions and prepare them for seating breaks and intermissions. The bartenders put on their uniforms, load buckets with ice from the ice machine downstairs, and prepare for the opening of the house at seven o'clock. Concessions too are being set up; everything must be ready before the doors open.

Backstage, the show's hair stylist has arrived and now begins to work on the wigs for the cast. She talks as she works, her teeth occasionally clamped around hairpins. Theaters, she says, have a variety of personalities. Some are definitely unwelcoming; others have an air of great hospitality. The Paramount? "It feels like home now. I feel like I belong here."

The wardrobe mistress and her assistants appear next. An hour before curtain time, the cast signs in, and the dressing rooms are immediately vivid with life. In one, an actress in a black slip leans toward a mirror and begins an elaborate makeup job that will transform her into a much older woman. In the room next to hers, someone closes the door and begins to sing scales. Down the hall, a group of people exclaim: an actor has just learned that his wife is pregnant; he plans to celebrate tonight. A woman steams past this group carrying coffee. Doors open and close; someone is dispatched to Wardrobe; the atmosphere is noisy, breezy, lively, but the serious business of dressing has begun. Onstage and in the wings, all is still silent, but from beyond the curtain the muffled sounds of the auditorium are dimly audible. An audience is beginning to gather.

A half-hour before curtain time, the stage crew arrives. There is an intense flurry of activity as the

Photograph by Gabriel Moulin

The Paramount opened with state-of-the-art equipment, including three Super Simplex projectors. Also from the earlier era is the DeLuxe double-slide effects projector (above right) from the Chicago Cinema Equipment Company. Slides were used for intermission advertising; they also flashed songs on the screen for sing-alongs. The double-slide projector made it possible to superimpose, or to fade from one slide to the other, and it was used in stage shows to produce clouds, sunsets, stormy skies and starry nights. The DeLuxe has been retired to the Paramount's fan room now, where it joins the ranks of some other venerable retirees. Today the Paramount's projection booth (above, far right) houses a Super Simplex XL 35mm projector with an Ashcraft Super High Intensity Arc projection lamp. Concealed behind it in this picture are two more Super Simplexes, with Strong Excelite 135 arc lamps, and an Eastman 16mm arc projector. The flexible pipe vents above the projectors release heat and smoke produced by burning carbons. At the opposite end of the booth are two Strong Super Trouper 'follow spots.' Each has an iris for dilating and diminishing the spot of light that is focused on the stage, a chopper for rapid off-on effects, and holders for colored gels to alter the hue.

This dressing room is one of fifteen. Two are at stage level, the rest in a wing above stage left. These spartan rooms are endowed for a time with the personalities and belongings of the performers who use them. During a show this is a lively and colorful environment, filled with energy and tension. Then the rooms revert to plainness, awaiting the next guests, the next performers to play the Paramount.

stagehands assemble and place the props, and a lot of noise accompanies this. Slam, crash, scrape, boom! —the audience's murmurs continue unperturbed, however. A stagehand is raised aloft in the cherry-picker to make a last-minute adjustment in lighting.

"Fifteen minutes, please. Fifteen minutes," says a voice heard backstage over the P.A. system. Downstairs, the musicians' cacophony increases; the wardrobe department's washing machine adds its slosh and drone to the sounds that swirl through all parts of the theater. In the dressing rooms, there is a body in almost every chair as the actors concentrate on their makeup.

At the five-minute call, there is no sudden panic. Actors begin strolling to their places onstage. The musicians are called to the pit, and the tympani can be heard tuning up. Wardrobe is called to replace a sweater; "Props!" someone shouts, and an umbrella is hastily and calmly repaired. The stage manager speaks quietly into a headset, and at a word from her, the overture begins.

Crew members are still onstage, but begin moving off now as the last actors take their places. All is suddenly calm and orderly, and as the curtain swings open, the last of the crew members glide into the wings.

Curtain

In the Grand Lobby, in the foyers and lounges, the bell warns patrons that curtain time is near. Black-garbed ushers lead them to their seats and hand them programs, but many theatergoers are too absorbed with the theater itself to concentrate on reading. The main curtain sparkles, a fantasy of gold and silver appliqué accented by the Columns of Light on either side of the stage, and the sculptured gold walls gleam. "What a treat!" a man says. "This is one of the great theaters in America."

As the lights go down, those who have been to the Paramount before look upward to watch them fade and change in the lace-like ceiling. A different kind of night falls now: the night of the theater, in which the curtain opens and all is just beginning. . . .

THE OAKLAND PARAMOUNT
Text by Susannah Harris Stone
Photographs by Roger Minick
Preface by Peter Botto

First edition Copyright © 1981
    by Lancaster-Miller Publishers
Second printing Copyright © 1992
    by Oakland Paramount Theatre

Paramount Theatre
2025 Broadway
Oakland, California 94612
(510) 893-2300

Typography by Jennifer Tayloe
Printing by South Sea International Press Ltd.
Design by Wendy Calmenson
Production by Richard Schuettge
Printed in Hong Kong

The Oakland Symphony Orchestra Association
    went into bankruptcy in September 1986

Permission is acknowledged for
the Gabriel Moulin photographs
from Pflueger Architects,
the Gabriel Moulin portrait
from Milton Pflueger, and
the floor plan and other photographs
from the Paramount Theatre.

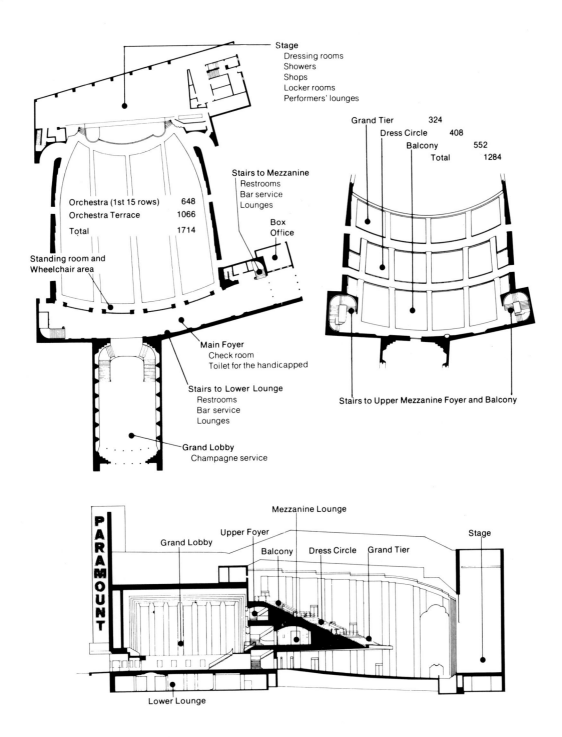

Stage
Dressing rooms
Showers
Shops
Locker rooms
Performers' lounges

Grand Tier 324
Dress Circle 408
Balcony 552
Total 1284

Stairs to Mezzanine
Restrooms
Bar service
Lounges

Box
Office

Orchestra (1st 15 rows) 648
Orchestra Terrace 1066
Total 1714

Standing room and
Wheelchair area

Main Foyer
Check room
Toilet for the handicapped

Stairs to Lower Lounge
Restrooms
Bar service
Lounges

Grand Lobby
Champagne service

Stairs to Upper Mezzanine Foyer and Balcony

Mezzanine Lounge

Upper Foyer

Grand Lobby

Balcony Dress Circle Grand Tier

Stage

PARAMOUNT

Lower Lounge

Acknowledgements

Achieving a fair degree of accuracy, even in as small a book as this, required the help of a large number of people. We would like to express our thanks to:

Peter Botto, the Paramount's general manager, for his unflagging interest in this project, for making himself available on short notice and despite a busy schedule, and for the hours he spent sharing his office, digging through archives, and climbing into every corner of the theater to show us what was there and how it worked;

Anne Cervantes, public relations director for Pflueger Architects, who repeatedly unearthed important drawings, photographs, and documents for us;

Luana DeVol, assistant manager of the Paramount and well-known soprano, for advice, assistance, and expert editorial aid which greatly improved the text;

Steven Levin, theater historian extraordinaire and projectionist par excellence, whose reams of carefully documented historical work on the Paramount provided the foundation for this book, and who has generously shared his research, his knowledge, and his time;

Milton Pflueger, brother of the Paramount's architect (and a prominent architect himself), for ferreting out facts, sharing recollections, finding—and lending—photographs and valuable historical materials, checking manuscript copy, and illuminating the spirit of an age with eloquence and humor.

Among the many more people who gave us invaluable assistance, we must first mention Jack Bethards, formerly the executive director of the Oakland Symphony and now owner of Schoenstein & Co., manufacturers of pipe organs. We are also grateful to Gordon Belt, program director for Merle Norman Cosmetics; Walter Buettner, stage rigging and renovation consultant; Marvin and Kay Burkman, theatrical drapers; Ina Crowle, Docent of the Paramount Theatre; Jacqueline Ellis, administrative staff assistant at the Paramount; Lamara Jackson, theatrical hair stylist; Lance James, dancer with the Oakland Ballet; John Pflueger, AIA, of Pflueger Architects; and Jim Roseveare, organist at the Paramount Theatre.

—*Susannah Harris Stone*
Roger Minick
July 1981

In reprinting this book, we required and graciously received the cooperation and assistance of the following individuals, to whom we express our deep appreciation:

Thomas R. Miller, Susannah Harris Stone and *Roger Minick,* with whose generous permission we are able to keep the Paramount story in circulation;

Richard Schuettge, publishing consultant, through whose expertise and patience I learned everything I wanted to know about publishing, and then some.

—*Peter Botto*
January 1992